Confessions of a Tiger Cub

Privileges of Asian Parenting Techniques from the Child's Perspective

Jenny Lin

Copyright © 2014 Jenny Lin

All rights reserved.

ISBN: 150245611
ISBN-13: 978-1502451613

DEDICATION

I dedicate this book to my parents, even though they probably don't
want this to be dedicated to them.
I'm supposed to be going to medical school.

And, in return for purchasing this book, I dedicate this book to you.
Here's a little something to add to your résumé.

There are accents on the e's. So it's legit.

CONTENTS

	Acknowledgments	i
1	Introduction: Author's Note	1
2	A Lesson in Asian Discipline: The Yin & Yang	5
3	Being Born a Young Tiger Cub	14
4	How The Tiger Cub Gets Schooled	18
5	The Infinite Struggles	24
6	Things You Do For College: Extra Curricular Activities	31
7	The Mirror Image	43
8	College	53
9	Picking a Major	63
10	Conclusion: The Privileges	72

ACKNOWLEDGMENTS

I acknowledge that I wrote this myself & only binge ate once. Or twice.

All jokes aside, a big thank you to my parents for raising me the way they did. Without them, I'd be dead. Literally.

1 INTRODUCTION: AUTHOR'S NOTE

If you are like me, you're used to skipping the introduction, especially if it is titled "Author's note." That shit isn't going to be on the test. See you in Chapter 2.

If you're still reading, thank you, you overachiever. We all heard Tiger Mom, Amy Chua's roar back in 2011, which highlighted the superiority of Asian parenting, but also illustrated the clashing relationship with her daughters. For some, her parenting techniques were seen as odd, perhaps even *too* cruel. But for my fellow Asian Americans who were raised by strict parents, let's be real, none of us were surprised. You've gone without dinner because you did not practice piano. You've sat staring at a wall for an hour, thinking about "what you've done." You've been hit by miscellaneous objects for bad grades.

The question stands, why am I writing this now? There are plenty of other critiques and books written on Amy Chua's *The Battle Hymn of The Tiger Mother*; all of which are written by grown-ass adults, and read by other adults. Simply put, I'm not writing a parenting guide.

I'm not here to tell a parent how to **train** their child to score a 2400 on the SAT. After reading Amy Chua's Tiger Mom article in the Wall Street Journal, I suddenly felt grateful for all my parents had done for me. The "meaningless" punishments resurfaced in various manners. The hours of piano playing taught me lessons I did not even know I was learning. The many times I felt myself wanting to excel, came from childhood roots. This book is a representation of my epiphany: the gold lining around the obscure punishments and pressure. After all, silver is for second place losers.

Although it was always difficult as a young child to understand why I was constantly punished for minute mistakes, I developed a strong work ethic and ambition without even realizing it. Operant conditioning works (look it up). Many people pigeon-hole Asian American women as "submissive," "quiet," "shy," "obedient," or "exotic." Okay, gross. Tiger Mom is proof of one who has completely shattered that stereotype. Welcome to the 21st century. Asian American women are strong, they're sassy, they're stubborn, they're loud (think of the last Chinese restaurant you went to), they're smart, they're aggressive, they might be bad drivers (sorry, I'm one of them).

It wasn't until after I graduated college, when I realized how special my own upbringing was. To clarify, not unique, but *special*. Hence, I'm writing this book at 22 years old because I know there are others out there who can relate. Being raised by Tiger parents drove me to share my experiences and provide a mode of understanding for our parents' actions. If you were or are currently being raised by strict parents and you're still alive, this is for you. Congratulations, you are a Tiger Cub.

How do you go from a Tiger Cub to a Tiger Mom? Do you grow up with baby paws clawing at your classmates for success? Probably. I don't remember a time when I have not been competitive. Even when I sucked at something, I was the worst at it, not second worst. When I took my license test, I failed the maximum amount of times. Hey, I never said I was good at everything, I said I was competitive. Starting at a young age, I was constantly competing. I have "Perfect Attendance" trophies lining the top of my bookshelf. Being sick never meant skipping school, unlike the average kid's dream. Being sick meant that I would miss a day of school and lose my award. Who the hell thinks like that? Oh right, me. The first time I cried at my elementary school, I had received second place at a Spelling Bee. Yes this is all true and bizarre, but this was my reality for a good chunk of my life.

Being born into an Asian American Tiger Den means being compared to your cousins, your friends, your parents' friends' children, your grandparents' friends' children, and pretty much everyone around you. You go to USC? Well, your friend got into an Ivy League university and is in the process of curing cancer, and suddenly your success becomes a quick failure. I can see how this would be disturbing for the vast majority of people. It was disturbing for me as a child. Why did I feel like I was never good enough for my parents, and in turn, myself? Going to college is going to college. But, in our world, going to college does not mean shit unless you go to a college your mom's aunt's second cousin in Taiwan has heard of it.

Now, I'm going to be honest, I am tired of people capitalizing on bringing up differences between races. I'm writing this not to solely confirm Amy Chua's parenting styles, but more importantly to show that although ludicrous, I have gone through a number of personal experiences that have shown me what it means to be a true Tiger Cub, and the sassy Asian American woman I am today. As I've mentioned before, this book isn't merely about what it's like being raised by Asian parents. Chances are, you are more than familiar. It's about reaching out to teens, young adults, and anyone who is currently in limbo, to keep striving to be the best you can be. Being ambitious, being competitive, being a "Tiger Cub," will lead you to be nothing short of an amazing individual. Let's be real, no one cares for average these days. When have you ever been satisfied with receiving a "C"? I hope never.

Because everyone has suddenly become an over sensitive pansy these days, I feel the need to place the following disclaimer before I continue: I do not speak for every single Asian American woman or Asian American family. The traits and experiences I describe are based on my own stories, my own love for story telling, and have nothing to do with race exclusivity. There may be experiences you relate to, stories you have heard from others, and lessons your parents have told you, but that's kind of the point. This book/novella is a symbol of appreciation for my parents, and a way to show you how to appreciate yours. With that being said, my stories, my book, my advice, are all written in my own tone of voice. I'm sarcastic. I don't take myself too seriously, and if you are easily offended, you might want to close this and peace out now. Bye.

2 A LESSON IN ASIAN DISCIPLINE: THE YIN & YANG

Asian discipline is a tricky subject. Actions that may seem abusive are actually out of love. While eating dinner one day, my mom decided to share some of her own childhood stories; her stories of having to walk to school, of having little to eat, of all the studying she had to do, you know, the typical tough life of an Asian story. She then proceeded to tell me about how my grandma used to hit her as a child when she received bad grades. "She used to use a clothes hanger, it was so scary." First of all, the image of my sweet, grandma smacking anything with a clothes hanger is hilarious, but also inconceivable. Secondly, the shocking turn of events was when my mom added, "Oh, aren't you glad I've never done that? You're so lucky." And that's when I realized my mom had amnesia.

Low key. It might have not been a clothes hanger, but there were definitely some rulers and hands involved. Despite being scared shitless, I once arrogantly told my mom I would call child protective services. Her response, "Okay, you'll lose your mom." Yeah, I clearly did not think that one through. However, none of this rings a bell for her. There has to be something that happens at pregnancy. It is scientifically proven that women are able to forget exactly how much pain they are in when they give birth. Hence, they have the ability to give birth to multiple children.

New theory, there is a gene that develops during pregnancy that links this sort of amnesia with disciplining their children, as proven through generations of studies. My grandma denies any disciplinary physical contact, as much as my mom does. But why do I distinctly remember nights when I was facing a wall, staring aimlessly at a bamboo plant for hours? Was I a panda in my past life? I wish. If I was a panda, I'd be ecstatic.

How to Behave In Public

You walk into a restaurant, and the first thing you hear is a wailing child. What is your immediate reaction? Mine is to look for the parents. There is nothing more in the world I hate, except for bees, than a crying child. But they're just children, you say. No, they're animals. Growing up, I was taught to never misbehave, especially in public. The first and last time I remember wailing in public was at our local K-mart. My dad and I went with the hopes of buying me a new bike. Not realizing how fortunate I was to get a bike in the first place, I started crying when things started to not go my way. I wanted the one with the pink streamers on the sides of the bike handles, instead of the boyish looking bike my dad was going to buy. The next thing I knew, I was walking out with dry eyes, a lecture, and no bike. Lesson learned.

Behaving in public and having manners are extremely important to Tiger parents. Of course there are also Asian parents who spoil their kids to no degree, but we don't care about the scum of the Earth. Their kids can go rot in their parent-bought Audis. In the eyes of a Tiger parent, when you are born, you become a representation of your mom and dad. My situation was no anomaly. Everyone in my family went through the exact same shit. During a family trip to Hong Kong, my younger cousin once got pulled out of a restaurant to get slapped outside for bawling in a restaurant. When my other cousins received bad grades, they knew they were in trouble when the blinds in their house started to shut. Although hitting may be seen as inhumane, it is definitely how we learned to behave.

Recently, I was studying at a Panera and was shocked to find these two little girls crawling around on the floor, meowing. Yes, meowing. So, for those of you who do not think kids should be trained like animals, here's exhibit A. As the two cats were sliding across the dirty carpet, I immediately asked myself, where the hell are these kids parents? Why would parents let their kids just slide around on the bacteria ridden surface of a public restaurant? Suddenly, her mom appeared.

Oh, thank goodness she's going to pick up her child and sit her down.

Plot twist, she hands her a piece of bread and returns to her booth, as she continues talking to her friend.

What is going on here? I immediately glared at the mom, and she smiled. Was this some sort of reverse psychology? Was she just treating her child like the cat she is? Because I'm pretty sure if I was sliding around on dirty floors and meowing at strangers, my mom would pick me up by the collar and throw me in the car. But to other parents, disciplining their child apparently means letting them do whatever they want because "they're just children." What people do not realize is that this extremely spoiled attitude is only going to get them in trouble later on. What happens when they're suddenly not allowed to do whatever they want in the real world?

You can bet they're going to be screwed. The lesson is you can't always stomp your feet and cry to get what you want.

Thanks Mom & Dad:

As much as I want to dedicate this whole section to bitching and moaning about how terrible my punishments were as a kid, I'm actually pretty darn thankful. Everyone with a strict Asian parent has similar stories, and it brings us together. It's the reason why I can write this book, and some of you will nod in agreement, while others probably have their own stories to tell. There were nights in college when my best friend and I would lie next to each other, exchanging stories of various ways we were disciplined as children. Each of these stories always ended with, "Yup, never had that happen again."

And that was the point. We never made the same mistake twice. Asian parenting methods may be seen as harsh by a lot of skeptics, and to be honest, yes they are harsh and very obscure. Some parents may tell their kids to not play with their food. My mom made me eat whatever was on my plate and I would sit there until it was done. This was the early beginning of when I started to learn how to swallow food like pills. Sorry not sorry, to the shrimp that had to be forcibly shoved down my esophagus. At least I provided some water for you to swim in. Happy travels.

While some parents may coddle their kids until they stop crying. My dad yelled at me to never to cry again unless someone was dead or dying. While some parents encourage feedback from their children, I was taught to never "talk back." If I talked back, a casket should be prepared immediately. Nevertheless until this day, I'm still not sure what "talking back" is, because I also got in trouble for not responding. There were lots of grey lines and I may not always have understood the reasons behind my punishments. But after talking to other friends who were raised the same way, I asked the following question: "Would you do the same to your future child?" The response is always, "Duh. How else are kids going to learn?"

So to my future animal children, it's for your own good, whether you believe it or not.

The Love From Asian Grandparents

With every couple of Asian parents, comes fully stocked with Asian grandparents. My grandparents are a continuing source of balance. They unceasingly cancel out the harsh realities of my parents' discipline, with love and kindness. There is no need for them to play "good cop/bad cop," because your parents are both bad cops. My grandparents have treated me beyond what I probably deserve. Though they were probably tiger parents, as confirmed by my mother, they were and are always going to be complete saints in my eyes.

The privileges of being a Tiger Cub include the overwhelming love from your elders and always being well fed. My earliest memory I share with my grandpa starts back in pre-school. My grandpa used to pick me up and pick some of the flowers from a fence that surrounded the entrance. I would laugh and point at the different flowers, helping him pick which ones I thought were prettiest. Years later, as I was pulling out of the garage, my grandpa stopped me, pointed his finger toward his garden, and asked, "Do you remember these flowers? They're from your pre-school." Frankly, I could not believe what I was seeing. With a big smile, he showed me the rows and rows of flowers he had planted with just a few measly seeds more than two decades ago. Just as my grandpa had spoiled me when I was younger, he had taken care of the flowers. The flowers are more than just a pretty decoration, they are part of the connection we will always share and cherish. Though Asians may not be the best at expressing their feelings, his unwavering love will always blossom through the flowers.

My grandma expresses her love in a different manner, through food. Like many Asian grandmothers, she is quite the expert on cooking our native cuisine. Not only does she cook for us, she goes out of her way every year to order these handmade moon cakes during the Autumn Festival. For those of you who don't celebrate, let me just say, it's a big deal. Trust me. Luckily, I live right next door to my grandparents and therefore we have a constant supply of delicious food. It's kind of a miracle that I'm not 200 pounds right now. Wait, not a miracle, it's definitely the Asian metabolism. Not only does she come by to share her cooking, she has been the one who has given me my allowance over the years. What? An allowance? How unheard of. My parents thought paying your kid to do chores was preposterous. I learned my lesson fairly quickly when I cleaned the whole house and even pulled out a vacuum to try and earn some money, and all I got in return was "good, you're doing something useful."

What is Love & Respect?

There is an apparent inability to show love in the traditional sense. Asian families don't hug and kiss every time we see each other. Well, at least mine doesn't. The last time my dad and I hugged, we were at my college graduation. The time before that was at my high school graduation. We show love through other actions. Love from my family and dare I say, most Asian families, comes in many forms and ways we may not even immediately recognize. You might have to wait for the flowers to blossom, the food to warm up, or just simply, grow up and realize what kinds of sacrifices your family has made for you and your success.

With love comes a lot of respect for my elders. Early on, I was trained to always greet my grandparents, aunts, and even family members that I didn't even know were related to me. There were times when I got in trouble for not saying "Hi grandma" loud enough for her to hear. There were other times I got in trouble for not properly greeting my relatives. Why was I getting in trouble for such seemingly minute things? Because they were my elders, and I had to address them with deference. I started to pick up the habit of constantly greeting people, even those who I may have been unfamiliar with. This made me upkeep a very outgoing and friendly personality, which is key to impressing your elders. As mentioned prior, being a Tiger Cub means you are a representation of your parents. If you can't be the best darn spokesperson you can be, you're fired.

In return for respecting your elders, they will treat you exceptionally well. My grandparents have shown their love in their own ways, and my parents have invested everything they have in me. But this investment plan, their 401K, their contract with you has the following in small print: I'll invest everything I have in you, but you sure as hell better take care of me when you start making money.

So yes, your parents are giving up everything they have for you. Their hard earned money goes straight into those textbooks, tuition, food, clothing…etc. But, when you make that money, you better believe it's going back to them. Most parents may kick their kids out of their house and tell them to go be independent at 18 years old. My parents and other Tiger parents will raise and support you at least until after you have graduated college. Why? So they don't get sent to a retirement home. Don't be rude.

Spoiled Kids: The Yin & Yang

I get it; a lot of parents want to spoil their kids. They are beloved creatures. They want to provide the best, and the best is often shown through material goods. Although the term "spoiled" depicts a Barbie princess who gets whatever she wants, being "spoiled" can also be a good thing. Say what?

Yes, one way to define "spoiled" is being too lenient or indulgent, i.e. your typical spoiled brat. However, "spoiled" also denotes being treated with great or excessive kindness, consideration or generosity. Although you may not have realized it as a child (I know I hadn't), you were actually always spoiled by your parents. Even though they denied you of that new bike you wanted or the newest game for your PlayStation, they treated you with excessive kindness, consideration and generosity in unorthodox ways. Let's face it; nothing we do is truly conventional.

How can anyone deny that your parents were not excessively kind when they cooked your favorite meal after you had won your latest competition? How can anyone deny that your parents were not excessively considerate when they pushed you to be the best because they wanted to ensure *your* success? And how can anyone deny that your grandparents showered you with greater generosity, when your parents were providing you with the proper discipline? As Tiger Cubs, our love from our family may come in the form of trying to shape us to be successful, but in that way, **we are spoiled**. We are spoiled by the excessive care and consideration we are constantly provided, even though sometimes it is a little hard to realize while getting hit by a ruler.

The Asian Tiger Cub life is filled with ups and downs, checks and balances, yin and yang. Growing up, I bitched a whole lot about my parents, but my grandparents softened all the punishments, all the lectures, by showing their continual support and affection. Our parents and grandparents have perfected the yin & yang system. Without the discipline and the hardships we have endured, we would not have recognized how lucky we are to be raised the way we were.

If I could time travel and pick how my parents would raise me, I still would pick my parents. Watching MTV's *My Super Sweet 16* back in the day I'll admit, I was uber jealous. Why did they have birthday parties that cost the same as someone's mortgage? But as I got older, I started to realize that these trust fund babies' goals in life are defined by what their parents give them materialistically, while our parents help shape our goals by providing us with life skills. So, while they're crying over their birthday cake not being the correct shade of pink, I'll be over here crying because I have too many choices for college.

3 BEING BORN A YOUNG TIGER CUB

The Birth of Competition & Confidence

The day you were brought home from the hospital was the day you were unwillingly inducted into the Tiger Den. Little did you know, all your aunts and uncles were already trying to see if you were cuter than their own daughter/son/Tiger Cub. You were. This will most likely make them unconsciously competitive and a little heated, but of course on the outside, they're beaming with joy for their new match. I mean, niece/nephew.

For the rest of their lives, they're on a mission to make their child smarter than you. And here, the Asian Arms Race begins. You start walking first. They start talking first. Your first word was mango. Your cousin's first word was dad. Cool. Sorry you were obsessed with mangos, you should've been more focused on your parents. You got the newest PlayStation. Your cousin was playing with a Gameboy. Let me throw in another example for the year 2000 babies. You got the new iPhone 6. Your cousin got the iPhone 6 Plus. Everything, whether conscious or unconscious, is a competition. You get the point, because you lived this.

Flashback. When I was younger, my (male) cousin and I were watching Titanic. I'm going to pause right here and let you laugh at how weird this is. You're welcome. My aunt had strategically placed us right in front of the T.V. as Celine Dion's *My Heart Will Go On* started blaring from their surround sound system. Confused, but clearly shameless, I started belting my heart out. Most likely off-key and definitely obnoxious, I sang so loud that it roused some sort of competitive spirit and my cousin started singing too. Remember, he's **male**. The house echoed with misheard lyrics and tone-deaf singing, but to us, we were battling it out for our shining moment.

15 years later, does any of this matter? Hell no. In fact, this memory is buried so deep that I had to watch a few thousand episodes of Dr. Phil to tap into this unspeakable moment. Embarrassment was never a factor. Being the best, on the other hand, was pretty damn important. The reality is, we both sucked, but we were confident.

P.S. If any one of my friends asks me about this in person, I will deny, deny, deny. I don't care if it's written. I don't know the words to *My Heart Will Go On*. I don't cringe when a drunken girl sings it at a karaoke bar. Who's Celine Dion?

Moving on, in early elementary school, I decided that I had to be popular because to me, being popular meant you were the best. Yes, decided. I wanted to be well liked by everyone. I wanted to have minions. Both of those thoughts and goals probably contradicted each other, but I soon developed this unbelievable ego. I played handball to the best of my ability and rocked at it. I played kickball, and managed to be good at it too. I had all the best Pokémon cards because somehow I thought they would gain some sort of value when I got older. I was wrong. By the way, does anyone want to buy Pokémon cards from me?

When light-up shoes were popular, I got light up shoes. I saw Regina George wearing army pants and flip flops, so I wore army pants and flip-flops. I hope someone gets that reference. I remember feeling upset when I couldn't get "Heelys" and saw my friend rolling around in them. After school, I took other children's rolling backpacks (those were the shit), built a fort, and threw backpacks at anyone who tried to enter. A year later, I cut a girl's hair and didn't get in trouble for it because the office staff thought I was so nice and cute. What the fuck? I had become Regina George by 8 years old. I probably could have made fetch happen. What gave me all this bitchiness, I mean confidence? I'm going to go with my parents constantly pushing me to be ambitious, outspoken, outgoing, sweet, and well mannered. Final answer.

A Lesson on Confidence

Now that I'm thinking about my past and getting all nostalgic, if I saw 8 year old me, I'd throw her out of a window. Who the hell does she think she is? More importantly, why in the world would people like me? I should've had **no** friends. Teachers should've hated me. However, when I was 8, there was no sense of embarrassment. Being confident was adorable to others. I stood on a table and belted Britney Spears songs, and my uncle's response was to name his first-born daughter after me.

Why is it that we lose that sense of confidence when we get older? Why is confidence often confused with bitchiness or cockiness post-puberty? Being well liked has a lot to do with being confident and happy with the person you are. Who's going to like you if you think you're an ugly duckling? Would you like a gross looking, unconfident, duck? Isn't that what the nursery story is about?

This is not to say that if you are not *physically* attractive, you are doomed. There are many people who are average or below average who radiate confidence. You'd be surprised. If you don't already know some of these species through experience, you can easily find them at your local bar on a Thursday night trying to pick up girls. They'll be wearing some sort of douche lord shirt that says "Beer Pong Champ," holding a drink in one hand, putting his other hand in his jean pocket, and trying to look uninterested.

A Note on Male Confidence from a Female's Perspective

A few years ago, one of my best friends and I were talking about boys. Typical, I know, shut up. But here's the kicker, we were talking about ugly boys. Like literally subpar, and we're not talking golf scores here. However, this sub-par looking Neanderthal had some inexplicable quality. He had tons of friends, he was the life of the party, and something drew us both to him. It was probably 50% alcohol, 50% his ridiculous amount of confidence.

The "something" about him was that even though he was not attractive, he owned every part of his personality. It made us curious. How does he have so many friends? Why do girls like him? Why do I feel like I secretly want this ugly dude's approval? I'm going to go with the fact that he harbored confidence he had developed as a child, the shamelessness, and the ability to carry himself.

Success in any field starts with confidence. Disclaimer, being shy and being introverted does not mean you don't have confidence. Who cares if you're a little quiet? I don't, if you can convince me why you're awesome through your work and your actions. This isn't a lesson on how to be outgoing; it's a lesson on the importance of confidence. I have plenty of introverted friends who kickass at what they do.

4 HOW THE TIGER CUB GETS SCHOOLED

I'll be the first to admit that my education and my background are slightly abnormal. Most Asian kids these days receive a public school education, and if their family can afford it, some tutoring on the side. The cost of education pretty much requires a family member to go deep into the black market and sell an organ or two. But, until college, my family had scraped by to provide a private school education for me.

Starting from pre-school, I never experienced what it would be like to be in a classroom of 40 people. My classes were always filled with 15-20. I was constantly placed in schools where academics were stressed beyond belief, but nothing seemed out of the ordinary. It wasn't until college, when I heard plenty of other experiences from my peers, that I realized not everyone's schooling was as competitive as mine.

What do you mean you didn't have a college counselor? Wait, your high school schedule wasn't designed like a college schedule? Your field trips weren't a weeklong and you didn't get to go to Argentina?

That last one may be a stretch, but I started to realize I was a privileged Tiger Cub. Suddenly, all those years of bitching about my school developed into intense guilt.

Before I continue, let me clarify: my parents are far from your typical wealthy Asian family. They're not Taiwanese ballers who roll around in piles of money, and they definitely do not spend the money we have frivolously. Growing up, our house was probably half the size of most of my classmates' houses, and we used coupons for almost everything. If it wasn't on sale, chances were I wasn't going to get it. With that being said, my parents always saved for my education. Sure they could have spent all that extra money on nice cars, designer clothes, and a better house, but they invested it all in me. I'm a selfish bitch and I didn't even know it.

Lesson here is, don't have kids unless you're willing to spend money on an unappreciative brat.

From kindergarten to 3rd grade, I attended a co-ed elementary school. I mention co-ed, because for the rest of my education, I was thrown into an all-girls school. We'll have to get to that later. My co-ed elementary school included experiences that are truly priceless. Just kidding, it included experiences that cost my family a kidney. Definitely not priceless.

Remember that cute little anecdote about me being a bitch at 8 years old? That happened, but I was also extremely on top of my schoolwork. In 3rd grade, my teacher trusted me to grade other people's homework, so you best be nice to me. I was a power hungry little kid, but more importantly, the school nourished my competitive spirit. There were constant speech competitions, spelling bees, and awards for academic excellence. And, I managed to win every year I was there.

Pause, before you shut this book, don't worry I'm not writing a memoir about all my success. These are merely minor details to elucidate the way I have been raised. I was taught that trophies = prizes. If I memorized 100 words and learned how to spell them correctly, I could get that new Pokémon game. If I stood on stage, in front of parents, my peers, and administrators, and recited stories in Chinese and won, I could pick out my next toy.

The reward system worked throughout my whole education because I was a greedy beezy. I was constantly looking for different ways to win competitions and prove to my parents I was worthy of my next gift. My cousins would frequently call me spoiled, not realizing how much work I was putting in to earn these toys. On the other hand, I'm pretty sure this reward system is also what almost made me bankrupt at Dave & Buster's recently.

How so? I found an inexplicable desire to win an outlandish amount of tickets to get an iPod Nano, iPod shuffle, and pretty much whatever else I wanted, instead of just buying it. And besides the low-key bankruptcy, it was worth it. There is nothing more satisfying than knowing you worked hard for what you earned. You want to hand me an iPod for free.99? I'd probably think you were crazy. Nothing amazing ever comes easy, or as my mom always says, "There's no such thing as a free lunch."

My work ethic from an early age translates into everything I do, and I truly have my parents to thank for that.

To be clear, my experience at my new school from 4th grade-12th grade could be another book on its own. Mid-way through 3rd grade, I remember my mom walking me into a small classroom to take a test. The classroom had folders dividing the desks, nothing out of the ordinary. She explained it was some sort of placement test, but at that point, I was already used to taking a bunch of random exams. It was another normal Saturday morning. The test was designed to evaluate your intelligence, at 8 years old. The test was also designed to evaluate whether I was smart enough to attend the school. Yes, I had to take a test to get into a school that included English and math sections. Sound familiar? No lie, it was pretty much a mini-SAT for elementary school kids.

As the test began, I remember sitting there staring at the math problems. Were these a joke? Why are there pictures? I started double-checking all my answers because I had finished with half the allotted time still remaining. Needless to say, I aced it. Why was the test so easy for me? Was it because I was a genius? HELL NO. I put that in all-caps because I'm nowhere near a genius. If I were, you bet I would be designing the next Facebook and not writing this book about being raised by strict Asians. Was it because English and math came easy to me? Nope. Okay then, what made the test, designed to be challenging, a breeze?

It was my mom. Somewhere in there, is a "your mom" joke. I'll leave that up to you.

Ever since I was younger, my mom bought countless math and English workbooks that were always one grade ahead of my current level. During summers, I would be filling out homework packets that she would design for me. While others were outside having water balloon fights, I was calculating the volume of water in a balloon.

While others were watching T.V, my mom had me read news articles and summarize them everyday. Not only would she buy extra workbooks, she was also extremely clever and thought about every single way I would try to get out of doing my homework. There were times where I would flip to the back of the book to find the answer key ripped out. There were also times where I tried to track her like a nosey dog to see where she had hid the answers, only to find an empty toolbox. For years, I was convinced she was a spy working for the F.B.I. But for years, I was also forced to try to do my additional homework to the best of my ability.

So, when it came time to test for school, nothing was too challenging. I had learned it all before. Not only was I seemingly "smart," I was also fairly outgoing due to the confidence and competitiveness my parents had instilled. Attending my previous elementary school, in which teachers and administrators loved me, I was never shy around authority. Therefore, it was no surprise when I aced the interview portion and even had the balls to ask the interviewer, "Why should I go here? What's so good about this school?" Though my mom was flaming hot Cheetos red with embarrassment, clearly the interviewer thought I was a riot and I was admitted shortly after.

Now what? I've made it into this "exclusive" private school. Cool. This meant absolutely nothing to me for the longest time. In fact, it wasn't until after I graduated college when I started to appreciate my elementary school to high school education. Not only did I ignore the significance of my private school education, I actually started to low-key hate my school and was completely ready to graduate by my senior year. You'd think I'd bitch about it being all girls, but no. All girls meant that I could put on a uniform, no make up, yell for a tampon, and run out of the door looking like a disheveled cookie monster.

So there are pros, but at what cost? Let's talk about the price. For one, my parents could have *literally* bought a new car every single year that they put me through school. I know I've joked a lot and included some satirical portions in this book thus far, but I'm not kidding when I say, this school was fucking expensive. And the saddest part for my parents was that I would complain all the time as though money for us just came raining down on the daily.

But here's the other thing, my parents never let me know exactly how much money they were spending on my education, while I was in school. It wasn't until a lot later, when I really found out what they were sacrificing for my education. The number of hours they had to work. The exhaustion they went through. The 30-minute drive to my school to drop me off before work and after, one way. The constant need to save money for me. Told you, don't have kids. They suck. For future reference, how can I adopt an adult?

5 THE INFINITE STRUGGLES

Lower-School & Middle-School

All right, now it's time for the nitty gritty. Remember when I said I used to ace school and everything was a breeze? Okay, now let's throw 29 other kids who also were equally excellent in their previous school. For a while I realized, holy shit, I'm not smart at all. I'm actually pretty average. And, that competitive part of me became increasingly frustrated. Can I just say that my school's mascot was a *tiger*? How appropriate. I was used to things at school being easy for the longest time, and suddenly my whole environment started to change year by year.

If I were to describe the environment with only a few words, it would be "passive aggressive." Just think about it, at 4th grade, you and 29 other children are split up into 2 classrooms. You have all taken the same test, passed the same interview, and now you're sitting next to each other thinking you're the shit. Guess what? You're not. I remember I was so nervous the first day; I didn't even bring a pencil. The girl next to me had 12. I was going to pee myself. Okay, not only are there 29 children, there are 29 other *girls*.

There's been a joke going around the Internet recently, "If women ruled countries, there would never be any wars, just a bunch of countries not talking to each other." That pretty much sums up school.

Of course as always, you had the exceptions. There were girls who were remarkably talented at sports, music or theater, but maybe not so amazing at school. We'll call them the "talents." But then, there were girls who you knew were smart as fuck, the "smarties." Original, I know.

School was divided in lower, middle, and upper school. Lower school was from 4th-6th grade, in which la-dee-dah, my mom was still having me do a bunch of extra homework and I was doing pretty well. Middle school, same shit. But, there comes a time, where Lakewood or Spectrum run out of books for children, and that time is high school.

All throughout lower school and middle school, I started to get pretty adjusted to my new all girls jungle situation. My school had us pick up an instrument in 5th grade and a foreign language in 6th grade. It didn't matter that you spoke a foreign language and played another instrument at home. You'd pick another one. So here I was, a little elementary school kid, learning to play violin and speak Spanish. Luckily, I picked up language and instruments fairly easily, and actually kind of enjoyed it.

Fast forward to high school. The key thing to remember here is that, although I made friends, we were still in a competitive environment and now there's a new ball game: the SAT and getting into college.

High School: High Key Struggles

While other high school students were worried about what they were wearing to homecoming and their plans for the weekend, I was panicking about college. Shut up, I'm a nerd.

Our school prides itself on being a "college preparatory" school. Yes, in 3rd grade, my mom and dad sent me to a college preparatory school. By now, I'm sure you see how much my parents put into my future success. In high school, everything started to matter. What happens when stakes are high, but there are no more prep-books that my mom can buy? Not to worry, I got sent to after school tutoring, summer school, all on top of my extra-curricular activities and lack of social life. Were my friends going through the same thing? Yes, my Asian friends were. My school might have been 60% Caucasian, but the 8-10% of us Asians were busting our ass trying to get to the top…quietly.

I say quietly, because no one really had any clue how smart our friends were. We had a vague idea, but no numbers, no grades, so pretty much nothing to base our perception of each other. We all had the common goal of getting into, of course, Stanford or any of the Ivy League Universities. P.S. Spoiler alert: Screw you, Stanford. Still bitter. Our high school provided college counseling, held seminars, and pretty much guided us throughout the whole process in the hopes that we would end up at a top-tier school. Why do they care? They have a reputation to uphold. Why do we care? Because we are prizes for our parents to show off if we're successful. It's really a win-win.

To be frank, I resented my mom for constantly pushing me to be at the top of my class. To be put through summer school, taking SAT prep classes, going to tutoring after track practice, spending time practicing an instrument you hate (a.k.a. piano), on top of being expected to volunteer, and do your homework for school, was **torturous.** But, what was even more torturous was the experience of not receiving Latin honors, realizing my unweighted G.P.A. was not within the top 20% of my class. Death was upon me.

My parents were furious to say the least. The tiger rage came out. I heard it all. "How are you going to get into college like this?" "When did you get so dumb?" "I think you need more tutoring." "Why did you get a B+ in art?" "How come other people have 4.0s and you have a 3.85?" Yes, a 3.85 was not in the top 20% of my class. The top 20% came down to the hundredth and thousandths decimal places. Keep in mind, these are unweighted G.P.As, placed on a 4.0 scale instead of 5.0, and do not account for any advanced placement classes. To also put this in perspective, an A- was a 3.67, a B+ was a 3.33 and a B was a 3.0. I got one of each, total. When I got my first and only B in high school, I cried, and I was led to believe I was going to end up at a community college.

A word on community college: I have absolutely nothing against community colleges or California State University (Cal State). Community college is a wonderful opportunity for those to receive an associate's degree in something and start a career, or get their general education requirements out of the way before transferring for a lower cost. I also understand a good majority of the population actually just graduate high school and move on with their lives. But, I'm not here to tell you about the majority. I'm here to describe the life of a Tiger Cub, and I'm going to tell it as honestly as I've been doing thus far.

Community college and Cal-States were unheard of at my school. We may have been called a "college preparatory" school, but it should have been called "Top college preparatory" school. Our college counseling sessions never included how to apply to a community college, or a Cal State University. For the "talents," they aimed to go to schools that were top in their field, i.e. swimming or soccer. For the smarties, your grades better be on point. If you were to Google "(Insert my school name)'s current average SAT score," you will find that it is 2140 out of 2400. To put things in perspective, the national average for 2013 was 1498. I'm not saying everyone at my school has an exceptionally high SAT score, but I am saying that clearly we all push each other to some degree to be the best. It wasn't just the mere 8 Asians pushing up the average; remember, my school is about 60% white. But here's the thing: when I scored a 2120 on my SAT, I was embarrassed. I was disappointed because my best friend had scored over 2300 on her second try, and here I was on my 3rd try barely hitting the average for a lot of the colleges I was looking at. That should give you a sense of where we were all aiming to go.

Once again, my parents were not happy despite my 100-point improvement with each try. "How could you do so badly again?" "How are you going to get into an Ivy League school with that?" "Wow, I wasted so much money on you." "You should've just gone to public school, you're not smart enough." Pretty much the best things you can hear when you already feel miserable. But, that only made me angry and I wanted nothing more than to prove to them that I was still able to get into an amazing college.

And then, I got rejected from Stanford. Until this day, my mom still talks about how sad she is about this. I've already graduated college, and it still haunts me. Great. And now that their football team got miraculously better, I literally have nothing to say.

But, I'll rewind. The day I got rejected from Stanford, I also got in one of my bigger car accidents. Like I said, I'm not a good driver. I had gone to the hospital to turn in my badge for volunteering, and as I got out, it started pouring. It was my first time driving my grandma's 1999 Sentra, and I had no idea what to do with all the fogged up windows. I stupidly started the car, turned on my windshield wipers, and started driving. Within minutes, I realized I couldn't see at all anymore. I turned on the defroster, the hot air, the cold air, but nothing was working. This old car was about to kill me. I was going to die. I made a left turn and found myself on top of train tracks. I got out, rain was pouring, and literally nothing was romantic about this rain scene.

Calling my dad, he quickly told me to call the police. Blurry car headlights and sirens blared toward me. That was the first time I had to take a sobriety test. That was the first time I told someone, other than my parents, I had been rejected from college. That was the first time someone asked if I was suicidal. I asked if this was the first time someone had crashed onto the train tracks. It was. Oops, I shut a train station down. It seemed like I literally had nothing going for me, except I was first to land a car on railroad tracks. Yay, me.

Now, let's take a quiz.

What was the first thing my mom said to me as she saw me?

- A) How could you be so stupid?
- B) Are you suicidal?
- C) Is this because you didn't get into Stanford?
- D) Are you okay?
- E) Everything but D.

If you picked "E," you are one step closer to becoming a tiger mom/dad. Luckily, my dad still had some sanity and made sure I was okay, before asking "C."

Do you "C" how much Stanford mattered to my parents?

Do you "C" how much I disappointed them?

Do you "C" how no matter what college I ended up at, I would be forever haunted by this?

6 THINGS YOU DO FOR COLLEGE: EXTRA CURRICULAR ACTIVITIES

A Lesson On Extra Curricular Activities Seemingly Ruining Your Life

You probably already knew this would be a section somewhere in the book. To be honest, I actually dreaded writing this section because it's bringing up a host of bad memories and semi-regrets. If you were raised a Tiger Cub like I was, you probably hated 80% of your extra curricular activities, but you were told by your Tiger parent that A) you had to do it for college or B) it's for your own good.

Chinese School

If I had a dollar for every time I tried to fake an illness to avoid going to Chinese school, I'd be rich. Every Chinese speaking kid was enrolled, and I'm pretty sure every kid hated it. First, it was extra school. Second, the teachers were Asian, so they're not afraid to yell at you. Third, if you get yelled at and you complain to your parent, your mom or dad will probably thank the teacher. And this is just the beginning.

What Chinese school really taught me was how to cheat efficiently, because in order to score high, you had to keep up with every other kid who was also cheating. In order to not get slapped with a stick, you need to pretend you know what's going on by acing your tests. Chinese school was survival of the fittest cheater. There were the pros, who were able to hide their answers in the dictionary without getting caught. There were amateurs who wrote on their shoes. I blame all the cheating on the pressures of doing well in Chinese school. These classes were pretty much run by Tiger parents. Just as your yelling mom dropped you off, your teacher was now yelling at you to read in front of the class.

Here's the kicker: Although I'll never admit it to my parents, I actually regret not trying harder in Chinese school. While our parents thought we were learning, we spent our time trying to play the system. We thought we were being clever, but I'm going to admit to my own stupidity. Learning a language at young age is much easier than it is as an adult. Although I was never officially taught Taiwanese, I picked it up at an early age because my parents spoke it when I was growing up. Your child brain is a sponge. Your adult brain is a rock. We wasted our child brain on cheating methods.

Of course I'm not implying that all kids cheat in Chinese school. This is merely my own experience. However, through many conversations with other friends who have gone to various Chinese schools, we all turned out the same way. You can tell us to write the following words: fire, me, you, her, good, and we'll ace it. We can get by with our colloquial Mandarin or Cantonese with any given situation. But, tell us to read you a newspaper or even the menu at a Chinese restaurant, you might as well be asking a blind person to drive.

If you asked me 10 years ago if I thought going to Chinese school was a privilege, I'd laugh so hard while clapping my hands like a seal. But now, I'm paying for it. In any job these days, speaking a second language is key. If you look Chinese/Taiwanese, you better speak the language. It's embarrassing that my Spanish is better than what should be my native language. Instead of writing answers on my shoe, stuffing answers in my dictionary, I should have been spending that effort on actually learning the material. Recently I started to use my pinyin keyboard to text my parents. Why? Is it because they don't understand English? Definitely not.

Is it because learning Chinese was actually important? Yikes. Yes. Although it may seemingly ruin your weekend now, you won't be an embarrassment to your race later. I'd say that's a pretty fair trade. Sorry to say this, but once again, your parents know best.

Summer School

For some people, summer means nice weather, beaches, and playtime. For me and my fellow Tiger Cubs, it meant summer school. Before I continue, there are two different types of summer school, and we need to make sure we're on the same page.

Type A summer school: Oh shit, you failed a class in school. Now what? Instead of getting kicked out or pushed down to the lower grade, you have another option. Yay for you. You get to take summer school to make up for not studying hard in the first place. So pretty much in this case, you're retaking a class you already took. Um. Okay. That sucks.

Type B summer school: You thought type A sucked? Think again. In this case, you have excelled all year. You've turned in papers on time, you've studied for those algebra tests, you've made sure to do all the extra credit, and what do you get in return? Summer school. Are you in the same boat as the person going to Type A summer school? No. They're in a sinking boat and they've been given a lifeboat for a second chance for survival. You're in a boat, cruising along just fine, when all of a sudden you're about to hit by a giant iceberg.

Before hitting that giant iceberg (yes, you've turned into the Titanic now), you need to steer at full speed and boost yourself ahead of the curve in order to stay afloat. Instead of a time filled with bliss, you're suddenly thrown a bunch of obstacles. But you go along with it, because guess what? You're not ready to share some life raft. Jack can freeze to death. Is it still too soon?

But what exactly is the iceberg coming your way? It is your fellow smartie competitors. It is the B you might receive in school. It is your parents' nightmare. Any of the aforementioned options will pretty much result in your drowning, so I'd say this iceberg metaphor is awfully fitting. Luckily, your parents are way ahead of you, and they'll start to navigate you toward advanced courses.

P.S. If this metaphor was too abstract to follow, go back to high school.

So, what are some summer classes you can expect to take?

Option A: Your Next Level Math Class

After "graduating" from 8th grade, I landed myself in Geometry Hell. Why geometry? Because it would get me ready for my freshman year math class. Truthfully, I don't remember a time where I have ever felt so miserable in my life. That includes the first time I realized I would get cramps every month. Geometry Hell was every single day of summer, for multiple hours. MULTIPLE. First of all, when did geometry become something more than identifying shapes? Can we go back to that? It also didn't help that suddenly math got really hard for me.

What I learned that summer: If a=b, then b=a. If a=b and b=c, then a=c. If summer school = death and death = hell, then by the transitive property summer school = hell.

But seriously, why was I spending so much time and effort proving why a triangle was a triangle? Also why were there so many weird acronyms? SSS, SAS, ASA, AAS, AA, SSS, SAS, if this were a game of scrabble, I'd be screwed. SOS were the only 3 letters that mattered to me.

It didn't help that I was in a class full of other Asian Americans who had been shoved in here by their parents. It didn't help that the teacher spoke at a thousand words per minute and drew shapes like nobody's business. It didn't help that it seemed like everyone else understood our teacher, while I was trying to draw a perfect circle on my paper. But most importantly, it *really* didn't help that they gave out grades and called your parents when you dropped below a B. I am still emotionally scarred by the day my mom picked me up, only to be notified by the secretary that I was <u>failing</u> summer school.

What happened next was a blur. I was publically shamed. So not only was I now failing my geometry class, I was getting owned and everyone was around me. The only upside was that if I were to get killed, I'd have a host of witnesses.

Option B: Test Prep Class

Now, we have the infamous test prep courses. The SAT was believed to pretty much determine where you would go to college. There is some truth to that, but mostly disillusioned truths. You were to spend hours sitting in a classroom, take practice SATs, learn grammar all over again, peruse reading comprehension passages, and write essays, all for one score. Your parents spent thousands of dollars to send you to these courses, so if you didn't hit that 2100+ score, you were going to die.

So there you are, finding yourself in a classroom for 8 hours a day, while it's nice and sunny out. What's even worse is the fact that tons of these other students are socially awkward and also hate life. They don't want to be your friend. In fact, you might as well be enemies. During break time, you'll find yourself staring at the ceiling, choosing to do your homework (desperate times), or texting your friends. Everyone just wanted to get the fuck out.

Not only did my parents sign me up for <u>summer</u> test prep, the program I was in was 14 weeks long. 14 weeks meant that it continued into the normal school year. So right after school, I was picked up to go to SAT class. Oh, but it didn't stop there. Saturday mornings were test days. **Test days.** As if spending every other waking moment wasn't enough, you had to go in to take practice tests, wait for your score, get yelled at because the score was too low, and repeat the whole process.

Despite all of this, I'm a survivor and I lived to tell the tale. The tale might have been filled with complaints, but I can say that I did relatively well on the SAT. I can say that geometry was still hard as shit. I can say that even though these are listed as "options," they're really mandatory. They're points of investment for your success. Your parents are hoping that by throwing some money at you, you'll spit money back at them in a decade or two. So we might bitch a lot, but we can't say we aren't thankful for our parents. These classes were not strictly hell; they were opportunities that many other children didn't have. Yes this may start to sound like the speech about not wasting food because other people do not have the luxury to eat, but it's pretty much comparable.

Get up and thank your parents. You managed to stay afloat.

Instruments

Let's start with the most highly anticipated one: *piano*. I don't even know where to start. How about when I started? I chose to play piano because I was a fat ass. Let me explain. Back in 1st grade, a piano teacher held lessons at our elementary school and as a reward for doing well, kids would get a snack. So yeah, I joined piano because of a cookie. At first, it was all fun and games, and then the private lessons started. And before I knew it, a giant black thing moved into my home, the piano.

Soon, I was spending unwarranted amount of hours a week practicing songs I had no interest in. Week after week, I got yelled at for not practicing enough. Year after year, I took the Certificate of Merit (CM) exam, slowly crawling along to that prized advanced level. This was surely not uncommon. Slowly, I forgot that piano was an instrument people actually enjoyed playing. I became so brainwashed, at one point, my mom got so sick of hearing me complain, she told me to quit. My response, "No, I need this for college." Mind tricks, yo.

It was during one of my CM tests where I still remember the words of another tester. While wiping my sweaty hands on the hem of my black skirt, I made eye contact with an older girl. I guess I looked pretty damn miserable because the first question she asked me was, "Is your mom forcing you to play piano?" I replied, "How did you know?" All she said was, "You'll thank her later." I scoffed. Thank her? Please. Piano is the bane of my existence. I'll thank her when I actually get to quit.

More than 5 years later, as I'm writing this now, I'm finding myself a little bit conflicted. During college, I realized how cool piano could be when my non-Asian friends would play any song, out of the blue. What was this sorcery and how do I access this magic? I spent all my time learning how to play Mozart through muscle memory. I'd be perfectly fine with that, but muscle memory has a major downside. Playing a song with your muscle memory means when you lose your spot, you really lose your spot. Soon, you'll find yourself staring blankly at a room full of people at a recital, while your mom is mentally throwing chopsticks at you. True story.

Although I was no way a piano master, I had an advanced certificate. It really makes me question the validity of this "advanced" certificate. My friends were certificate-less, but they were able to play any requested song. They were taught piano in a different manner, one that seemed to be more practical and fun. Instead of memorizing, they were taught to listen to enjoyable music and replicate the tones through the keys. Piano was a true hobby for them. As I listened to my friends play, I became increasingly frustrated. I also decided I should start selling frames that say, "I played piano for 12 years, and all I got was this lousy certificate."

Now I'm **sure** you're wondering what the privilege of being a Tiger Cub is, especially in this instrument case. After all, I just raged about how other people are so much better at piano. For a competitive Tiger Cub, admitting you are worse than someone is pretty devastating. What is so good about a piece of paper that validated all those painful hours? Let me break this down for you.

Next time before slamming your piano case, think about the following: How many times did you want to quit? If you were like me, it was literally every second of every minute of every hour of everyday. How many times did you want to run away from home because your piano was constantly staring at you? Countless. How many times did actually you quit before you reached the decided level of accomplishment? Zero. Why? Your Tiger parent pushed you to finish because it taught you to stay dedicated. You're not a quitter. Life isn't always about doing things you love, but apparently it's about excelling at something you might hate. Isn't that how people end up working office jobs?

If you can play an instrument you really hate for 12 years of your life, you can do anything. And yes, the same applies to violin, flute, or whatever your choice of instrument was.

My mom always emphasized that everyone needed a talent, everyone needed something special, and even though I was horrendously terrible at piano, I pushed through all of those levels. Piano was not my talent, and piano definitely did not make me special, but piano played a huge part of my childhood. Although I'll admit that it most likely didn't do anything for my college application process, I was taught never to give up. I learned something truly special through the endless hours of practicing, there is nothing worse than playing piano until you feel like you've developed arthritis at age 15. Plus, if you ever need something to fill in that little gap at the bottom of your résumé, throw in your certificate. Bitches love certificates.

Sports

Not only were you expected to play an instrument, you had to play a sport. Luckily, my parents let me order the sport-sampler before eventually picking a sport-entree to stick with. This led me to trying a whole host of sports including gymnastics, ice-skating, basketball, swimming, volleyball, soccer, tennis, and track. Here's the thing, they were all fun until 1) I got hit by something, or 2) I was forced to do it. If I could eliminate one of those options, I was happy with that. So, I picked track. No getting hit by balls, and I had made some close friends so it didn't feel as terrible. But let's be real, it was also a pretty strategic Tiger Cub move. Our team was so small, everyone was pretty much varsity. I knew my parents would be pleased, because "varsity" was the highest level you could be. The key Asian goal is to pick an extra curricular and get to the top, whether it was playing an instrument or a sport.

What sports are most common for Tiger Cubs? If you're a true Tiger Cub, you probably play or have played tennis. Tennis is great because you get to hit your competitors with balls if you develop the skills.

It's like a real life circus game. Tennis is also great for Asian parents to follow along because there are numbers that tell you who's winning and for the most part, it's an individual sport. If you play singles, you're a little screwed. Your parents have no one else to blame, but you.

Let's say you find yourself wanting to play a sport that's a little bit more bougie or "classy". If you're a bougie Tiger Cub, you'll probably go with something a little bit more exclusive: ice-skating. Tennis is to stretching, as ice-skating is to yoga. Ice-skating allows you to look more graceful than you probably are, and you get to buy cute outfits. The con of course, the cost. A pair of skates costs your mom an arm. A cute outfit costs your mom a leg. But, it's all worth it because you want to grow up to be an ice skater right?

Hell no. Here's the thing about sports in the Tiger Den: they're not meant for your career. You're expected to only be excellent enough to reach a certain level aka varsity. Why? Because again, everything you do is for college, not your actual life. Asian parents typically don't **want** you to become a professional athlete. In fact, if you were to tell most Tiger parents that you've been drafted for the NBA out of high school, they would have a heart attack. If you're thinking, "wow, my parents are so happy for me," you're in for a big surprise. Despite your seemingly successful sports career, your education will always come first. Think: Jeremy Lin still went to college, and not just any college, he went to Harvard. Sports are a vehicle for your eventual educational success. The talents at my high school were recruited for colleges; they used their sport or their craft to advance their education. For those of us who are on the smarties side, your parents are forcing you to play a sport so you don't look like a nerd. Be thankful.

Are You Done Yet?

You have a sport and an instrument that you are forcibly exceling at. You think you're on top of the world? Get off your high horse. Your extra curricular activities need to include another sport or another instrument. You need to show people you are versatile, not only can you bang on some keys; you can also use a bow. Not only can you kick a ball, you can hit it with a racquet. Now that I've leaked the not so secret truths of Tiger Cub success, what do you do to stand out?

I did what every normal child would do; I picked up two more extremely obscure instruments, the electric bass and ukulele. The lesson here is I need to get a life.

With my four instruments in hand and a varsity sport, you'd think I'd have no time for anything else. Please. We're not amateurs here. We can't forget the millions of hours spent volunteering at a hospital. If you didn't have some sort of volunteer uniform shoved into a bag, you were failing as a human. It doesn't matter if you don't want to be a doctor in the future, you are going to go to a hospital and help people. But again, how are you going to stand out? Pick another extra curricular activity. Do you see a trend? I've tricked you this whole time. This book is really a manual to land yourself in a psych ward.

In between your instruments, your sports, your volunteering, your grades, your AP exams, and your SATs, let's not forget to include the struggle to really stand out by earning awards. Whoever said high school was easy, was trippin' on drugs. Literally.

7 THE MIRROR IMAGE

Though my private school education may have been a little different, my parents' undying love and sacrifice for my education is not uncommon. Recently, I started tutoring a 10-year-old Asian girl in English. When I first received the call, I was a little bit shocked. Frankly, I was expecting a fob (uh, fresh off the boat) to be like "escoo meh, how much charge for tutoring?" Instead, on the other end of the line was an extremely eloquent man, who was requesting tutoring services for his daughter.

Let's back track. A few months earlier, I had put myself on this website called "University Tutor," thanks to some lovely advice from my best friend. She had experience tutoring high school students in basic biology, and recommended I try the same for English (keep reading, and you'll find out why I chose the most fail-major as an Asian). Anyways, playing into the "I'm so un-employed and I majored in a humanities" stereotype, I signed up expecting to tutor high school students, maybe even some freshmen in college.

Ok, now fast-forward to that phone call. This man wanted me to tutor his daughters, ages 10 and 12. For a lot of people, this is pretty surprising. As a 10 or 12 year old, you probably spent most of your days biking around, having a shit ton of fun, without noticing that the blinds were closed to your Asian neighbor's house. Inside, she was probably practicing piano or violin, right before doing her extra homework her mom assigned. Now, I found myself on the other side. Here's how the conversation went down, disclaimer: I might have paraphrased, and by "might have," I did. Can't get sued, ya heard?

Dad: Hi, I need a tutor for my 10 and 12-year-old daughters. They need major help with their English. They suck and I'm going to spend the next 20 minutes telling you why and what they need help with, while you sit there awkwardly agreeing.

Me: Oh okay, sure. No problem. I have plenty of experience helping children with English…because reading to children for a week felt like months.

Me in my head: Damn, these kids must be freakin' ESL or something. Why is his English so good? Hell yeah, employment.

Dad: Are you okay with picking up my kids? How was your experience in college? I see you went to a pretty name brand school. What did you learn as an English Major? What did you find the most rewarding? What is the most important thing you feel my kids should learn?

Me: Sure, of course. Whatever is most convenient for you! Being an English Major really opened up my options. It's so open that I need to pick up this tutoring job as a recent college graduate. Reading and writing are skills you need in real life because writing a 20 pager on horror philosophy my senior year was so influential and your daughters need to understand that to also get into a great college. Follow my awesome example.

Me in my head: Picking up your kids? I'm not your baby sitter. Can I raise my fees? What in the world did I just sign up for? Is this a phone interview? I'm not going to get hired. When can I hang up? I hate talking on the phone.

Dad: Great, I'll send you an e-mail with a briefing of everything we just talked about because this is super important and my kids are only on the honor roll and that is just not acceptable.

Me: Understood, being on the honor roll is for pansies. Let's get them on that Principal's award.

Moral of the story here is that Asian parents never change. Why is a father calling me about tutoring his elementary school kids and asking me how they can get into a good college already? Building a foundation is where it all starts. When I was younger, there were few days that I had to just run around and play. That was just frankly unheard of and completely ridiculous, unless you were a monkey or a low-life. I was taught that to excel in life, I had to do work when others weren't. I had to learn math and English at levels above my own, so I could always be ahead of the game. I hated every bit of it but now, every week, I see the girls go through the same thing. They finish up with their 8-hour school day, only to be bombarded with their mom's homework, tutoring, piano lessons, gymnastics, and every extra curricular activity possible.

Here's some insight into our tutoring session. These girls arrive at tutoring looking like exhausted raccoons, and I'm looking at them like…shit, I feel bad for you. Then, I sit down and they start to tell me about their day. I look at the clock, we're 5 minutes in and her mom is probably going to kill me if we don't start learning immediately. I divert her attention back to her homework. She sighs.

She tells me how much school sucks, I agree. I start every sentence with "yes, when I was younger" and age myself about 50 years. I tell them that it'll be worth it, because guess what, if you work hard now, you can go to college for free (what up, scholarship money?). I remind them of all the benefits. They care more about their snacks. I also care more about their snacks. I'm hungry. I tell her to pull out her homework, and for the first few weeks, they try to con me and tell me that they forgot to do it. Funny thing is, they don't know I tried to use that trick years ago. There are countless Chinese and piano homework sheets lying around, crumpled at the bottom of my piano bench that I simply "forgot" to do. I feel their pain, I "Elsa" it, and let it go.

Fast-forward, half an hour later, they're distracted again. I ask them if they understand, they nod. I ask them to explain it back to me, they can't. Frankly, they just don't care. They just want to tell me about the latest school gossip, their drama with their teachers, and I love every bit of it. I love every bit of it because these are moments of their "play" time. The ability to think of something other than school, the trust they have in me to tell me about all these things. But slowly, I realize that I'm not their friend, psychologist, or older-sister figure, I'm a hired tutor. I struggle between wanting to help them have fun and be children, and knowing that what their parents are doing, is ultimately the best for them.

Being a tutor for these elementary school girls has made me realize the difficulty of being an Asian parent. While her friend is waiting to get picked up by her mom and playing around, she is sitting there learning 15 new vocabulary words a week and getting extra quizzes (sorry, not sorry) outside of school. Nevertheless, I start to want her to succeed as much as her parents do. I start to care less that they're in elementary school and forget that they should be playing on the playground like the boys throwing a football right outside. With every quiz, I have a need for them to do better. I throw in anecdotes about all the times I had to stay in and study. They ask me if I had ever struggled in English as a kid, I say no. What kind of Asian struggles in school? I tell them about why everything they're learning is important…even though frankly, I was just as uninterested in "social studies" as a child. And for the record, as a 22 year old, all "social studies" means to me now, is the study of social-ness. So, if you're a fully functional social media addict, you're a social studies expert to me.

But, I digress. Transferring my instilled ambition, I try to spark an interest in these girls, which brought me to a major dilemma.

From an early age, I learned the importance of staying ahead, and these girls are a mirror reflection of my own childhood. There were tough times where I wanted to just smash all the keys on my piano, trying to create the most cacophonous sound. There were other times where I felt like my value was based on my grades. My childhood had its ups, when I got good grades, and its downs, when I got a B. Yes, a B. I understand how difficult it is to stay motivated in school at such a young age when college looms in the distant future, but I also understand how my work ethic as a child that my parents had instilled in me ultimately affected my study habits throughout my whole education.

What was most interesting to me was that the "uninterested" and easily distracted daughter actually had some competitive instincts. While reading her writing sample with the prompt, *Should Every Kid Receive Trophies?*, I almost died laughing. This so-called "unmotivated" or lack luster girl wrote paragraphs and paragraphs about how not to give everyone trophies. Trophies were for winners. She went so far as to say she would be **furious** if anyone who did not work hard got a trophy. For her, trophies are something to be earned, something for the elite. There was none of that "oh, A for effort" B.S., that children and parents alike throw around these days. Even as a young girl, she wants to be recognized for her hard work. She wants to stand out from the crowd. Her competitive spirit is evident through her inability to fathom the idea that everyone can receive a trophy. She acknowledges the concept of *deserving*, and therefore *rewarding* excellence. So, all this time, it wasn't that she was "unmotivated," she simply hadn't discovered the competitive nature of her education. Unfortunately for her, this meant that I became 10x more invested in her accomplishments.

And now, I have a problem. After weeks and weeks of uncompleted homework, followed by weeks and weeks of discussions with her mom, I didn't know whose side to be on anymore. I started noticing a trend. Let's now pause for a moment of silence, a part of me just died inside. Was she just impossible to work with? Was I wrong the whole time? The girl constantly gave me an excuse for not doing her homework. I was even low-key offended she didn't put more effort into her excuses. I had heard them all before. How? I muttered the phrases myself, only to be publically shamed in front of my tutors and teachers.

Here are some common excuses and tactics, that either you or your Tiger Cub Asian friend have probably used. These aren't your low-level "my dog ate my homework" excuses; this is some next level shit.

Tiger Cub Excuses

1) I can't find it! (Signal some sort of physical sign of distress)
2) OH! I didn't understand what you said I had to do.
3) What are you talking about? You only assigned me A, not B.
4) I guess I just forgot, I'm so sorry. (Insert some really depressing, puppy dog face)
5) I thought about it, but I didn't know what to write down because I wasn't sure.
6) My favorite: erasing homework problems that were circled and pretending they were never assigned.

With all of this in mind, #1-6 were used, alternating, on the daily. Girl, please. I practically invented these ridiculous tactics, and they are far from fail proof. I suddenly didn't feel any sort of sympathy toward her. In fact, I felt the complete opposite. I felt frustrated and irritated because I had believed in her. I wanted to tell her mom everything. How could she try to lie to me week after week? I THOUGHT WE WERE FRIENDS. After one of our sessions, in which, once again, she did not finish her assigned homework, she turned to me and asked, "Are you going to tell my mom?" Fucking duh. Oops, I mean "I can't lie to your mom, so I have to tell her that you only did part of your homework." At this point, I've lost every single ounce of patience. For her response, refer to #4. As cute as she was, she lost my trust. She tried to play me for the past 4 weeks, and I was not having it. Stop telling me that my nails are pretty. It's not going to work, anymore. Then, everything changed. Yes, I'm fickle. Get over it.

Her sister muttered, "Oo…remember what mom said? You're in trouble." Her response, "I know…"

Suddenly, I snapped out of my tiger rage of betrayal. What's going to happen to this girl? Just as I know all of the Asian homework excuses in the book, I also know of all, if not most, of the Asian punishments.

I asked, "Is everything okay?" Her response was cold, empty, and disheartening. It was as though I had just asked if someone had died, which in retrospect is pretty fitting. She explained that her mom had given her an ultimatum, if she missed one more homework assignment, she would have to drop gymnastic, one of the only activities in the week she looks forward to.

Shit.

At this point, I don't know whether to tell her mom or not. What if she is forced to quit gymnastics, but she could've secretly been the next Shawn Johnson? What if her mom finds out I didn't tell her about her daughter's progress? I carefully evaluated the situation by putting myself in both positions.

When I was around 11 or 12 years old, I cared a whole lot about school. I was taught to care, and I believed everything my parents scared me into thinking. However, this girl has a mind of her own. Although competitive, I was no longer sure if she translated that same spirit into school. She could care less about school, and no matter how many stories, how many lessons, how many times her parents yelled at her; no one could force her to care. Was she just a generally apathetic girl? No, I've seen her eyes light up when she talks about gymnastics, when she talks about ice-skating, when she talks about her friends. I find myself slightly starting to sympathize with her, as most elementary school children *should* be enjoying their extra curricular activities, should be having fun, and should have some sort of a childhood outside of a classroom.

Nevertheless, I also understand her Tiger mom's perspective. She wants what's best for her daughter. She's worried about colleges already. She's worried her daughter won't *ever* be motivated. She's worried that her daughter won't succeed. She's worried her daughter's work ethic now, will translate into failure later. She worries she won't be able to keep up with competition. She wants her daughter to have a secure future. She wants her daughter to be bright, intelligent, a standout. She wants me to tell her about her daughter's progress on a weekly basis, because she wants to see progress, not only in her reading and writing, but also in her ability to keep up with her work.

Spot a common theme? Worry.

I once yelled at my mom. That was my first mistake. I told her, "Stop worrying so much about me!!!" All three exclamation marks are necessary. They also symbolize a mountain of regret I had, as those words left my mouth. I've never seen her more hurt or more angry in my life. Her response was to stop cooking for me, stop doing my laundry, and stop literally everything I had taken for granted.

"Stop worrying? Okay. I'll stop caring." It was then, when I learned that "worrying" about someone and "caring" about someone are synonymous. Parents worry out of love, they act out of love, they care out of love, but as children, all we see is the aftermath of their worrying. The additional tutors that come in. The SAT English class you're forced to take, starting beginning of high school. The additional math classes they sign you up for. Chinese class. Piano lessons. All of this seems like punishment, until that day you end up with a scholarship to a great university. Team Tiger Mom all the way.

With that in mind, I told her mom, fully aware that she might cancel her daughters' gymnastics lessons. However, if she were a true Tiger Mom, she would keep that extra curricular activity going…for college. And sometimes, all it takes is a reality check. In less than a week later, her daughter was turning in her completed homework with exceptional penmanship. Even at a young age, she started to ask about my college experience, what she could expect, and even fought for a spot to go on a field trip to a local university. The lesson is, although often times it may seem like your mom and you are at war, in the end, you're both fighting on the same side for your success.

8 COLLEGE

Furthering Your Education

How many times have you watched a reality T.V. show or a live competition show and heard the following phrases from young teens:

"If I fail, I have no where else to turn. This is my last chance."

"I need this opportunity because I have no back up plan."

"If I don't impress the judges, I might have to give up on my dreams."

Yeah, that's what happens when you don't have a high school degree or a college degree. What happens if you fail? What happens if you don't have a back up plan? What happens if you don't impress the judges? Stop being a bitch and go back to school. Whether it is singing, acting, or any other artsy shit, you need to get your act together and get a degree. Why? How many artists make it big? What makes you think you'll be that one? But how many people earn a degree and learn to hone an academic craft and make 6 figures? I can tell you, it's more than the number of successful artists.

Your parents acknowledge how low the artist life success rate is and from an early age, you are led to believe that college is the only option after high school. As many sports I've tried, and as many instruments I've played, not once did my parents tell me, "you should practice and become a professional (insert art here)."

Fine fine, you'll go to college. Too bad any regular college is not good enough because your parents have set some pretty high standards. The result? You grow up being raised as an elitist college bitch, but that's what will get you ahead.

As discussed, Tiger Cubs have never aimed to attend a community college, or Cal State University. If it isn't mentioned top 25 in the U.S. News Report, our parents don't give two shits about it. Even if you're a Tiger Cub "talent," your skill better get you into an Ivy League University. Case and point: Jeremy Lin. Otherwise, you and your skill might as well be dead to them. You and I both know that rankings don't tell you anything about the actual school. Going to a top 10 university does not necessarily mean you'll end up with a six-figure salary. However, to Tiger parents, rank is everything because it increases your chances for success.

The idea of "choice" or "choosing" your college is pretty hilarious. If you didn't have a choice to be placed in a bunch of extra curricular activities and extra classes, what makes you think you'll have the *choice* of pursuing further education? Going to college is an immediate next step for Tiger Cubs. It is completely mandatory. Why is college important? Is it because your parents want you to continue to get a great education and prosper? Yes, that makes up about 10% of the reason. What's the 90%? Asian parents need to be able to share with their friends, co-workers, and family members, everything about you. And by share, I mean brag. And by brag, I mean humble brag. Tiger parents have mastered the art of the humble brag, but this requires you to actually be worthy of something. So, don't be useless.

The Humble Brag

What's a humble brag? If you're a Tiger Cub, you have definitely heard a variation of the following phrases:

"Oh, my daughter isn't that great, she *only* ended up at Brown."

"My son's internship is *only* paying him $15k a summer, that's nothing."

"I wanted my daughter to be a doctor, but now she's just the CEO of her own company."

"What's the point of being an engineer if they can't buy me a Mercedes yet?"

Get the point? Asian parents dumb down their kids' success, just in case your kid is more successful. Furthermore, out of common courtesy, you have to appear humble and unimpressed by your child. Unfortunately, chances are if you are the Tiger Cub on the receiving end, you are about to hear a mouthful from your own Tiger parent. "Did you hear that "X" got into Princeton? Why are you so dumb?" "She got into a top law school, and what are you doing?"

At first, you start to get defensive:

"So what? Princeton is so expensive."

"What'd he go for? A history major? So useless"

"Law school is for people who are boring," - Elle Woods' dad.

But your parents hear:

"Wow, I wish I was X."

"I'm so sorry I'm dumb as a rock and can't be as smart as X"

"I wasted all your money because I didn't get into Princeton."

No matter what you say, you're screwed because guess what? You lost in the Asian Monopoly board game. While they're complaining that they've hit Boardwalk, but can't buy a hotel yet, you just picked up a "Chance" card that sent you directly to Asian jail. Although the humble brag may seemingly appear modest, you can bet it's a form of bragging. If anything, it is the **worst** form of bragging. Not only are they showing off their genius child, they're acting as though everyone is up to par with their genius child and that their child is not special. It's really a lose-lose.

So, here's my PSA for humble braggers and successful Asian kids: Stop ruining my life. K. Thx. Bye.

"Acceptable" Colleges for Tiger Cubs

Ivy League University

Here is the normal list of the Ivy League universities in America: Brown University, Columbia University, Cornell University, Dartmouth College, Harvard University, Princeton University, University of Pennsylvania, and Yale University.

Here is the Asian list of the Ivy League universities: Harvard University, Princeton University, Yale University, Caltech, MIT, and Stanford University.

Where'd all the top liberal arts colleges go? Why are there two different lists?

Literally nothing else matters because Chinese newspapers do not report about any other schools. When one of my best friends a.k.a. one of the smartest women I know, landed herself at Cornell and graduated at the top of our high school class, her mom called my mom and said the following, "Ugh, she graduated #2 in their class and *only* ended up at Cornell." Where did I end up? Well, I wasn't in the top 20% of my class, so let's just keep that in mind for now.

Tiger Parent Perspective (TPP) on Ivy League Universities:

Harvard, Princeton & Yale = You are so beyond intelligent. You'll either become the next Bill Gates or Mark Zuckerberg, or you'll marry one. No matter what, nothing can go wrong if you land yourself there. You probably graduated high school with a 4.0, scored a 2400 on the SAT, cured cancer, built a robot, and turned into Oprah, while campaigning for the president. You'll make every other kid feel like shit, but you can wipe their tears with your millions in the future. Good job, you humanitarian you.

Caltech & MIT= Smartest nerds alive. It's not rocket science. Enough said.

Stanford = If you're a California native, this is your holy grail. Stanford is the "Ivy of the West Coast." You're exceptionally smart, but there's also something unique about you. Bitches love unique. You're going to equally make every other Stanford reject child hate you. No biggie.

What each school says about you is also what your Tiger parents want others to see. Ivy League Universities are important because college is an understood, golden prize of their success. Not your success, *theirs*. It displays they're alpha over other parents. They need everyone to know they have put in so much effort, money, and time to raise an amazingly smart child. So if you're crawling along, going to a no-name school, you can be sure you're about to feel really bad about yourself. To your parents, going to an Ivy League University means you can probably support them in the future, no problem. In fact, you'll be even more successful because you'll be surrounded by equally smart people. College pretty much acts as a filter for stupidity. But, what happens if you end up somewhere else? Are there other options for the "not so smart" Tiger Cubs out there?

Kind of.

University of California, _____

I left a blank there, but who am I kidding? Unless that blank is filled with "Berkeley" or "Los Angeles," you've failed. And, if you've landed yourself at UC Berkeley or UCLA, you've merely won the silver prize of Asian success. Again, meh to silver.

Checkpoint: Before you throw this book against a wall because you feel personally insulted and I've hit some sort of nerve…let's get a couple things straight. Every school I have mentioned so far, are schools that Tiger Parents believe to be certain keys of success. These may or may not be my personal beliefs, but I do have plenty of family and friends who ended up at different universities who are doing pretty damn well. Come on, I'm writing a book, and one of my best friends is working in Australia. I don't care where someone goes to college, as long as they hustle or are able to find their passion. In the end, success is of course, based on the individual. If you went to Harvard but you are a total asshole, no one's going to care about you. If you didn't even go to college, but are extremely smart, think *Good Will Hunting*, you'll live a far more fruitful and meaningful life.

TL;DR: College is merely a marker for other parents.

With that being said, I'm not here to write you a fruity little paragraph about success in real life. I'm here to talk to you about success in the Asian Tiger world. Let's talk about my experience with the silver prize aka the consolation prize for not getting into an Ivy League university.

But first, *TPP: What does each UC say about you?*

UC Berkeley & UCLA = You'll live another day. Look, you're fairly smart and your parents won't be totally embarrassed to tell their friends. However, this will not excuse you from the comments here and there about how your peers were admitted to better universities. Furthermore, prepare yourself for a host of other Tiger Cubs that are about to try and eat you alive.

UC San Diego = 6 different colleges in one? Too confusing.

UC Davis = Farmer.

UC Irvine = You're not smart enough for UC Berkeley or UCLA. You low key want to be a fashion blogger. Your parents are probably rich and they'll be disappointed, but they'll get over it. Maybe.

UC Santa Barbara = You're hot, but your smarts aren't.

UC Riverside = You're about to get boiled alive by the weather and you deserve it.

UC Merced = What's a Merced? Unless Merced is followed by "-es" and you magically land your parents a new Mercedes, you suck.

What happened to me?

I had the luxury of choosing a college by location and did not apply anywhere out of state. Who can pass up sunny California? I applied to six schools: Stanford, UC Los Angeles, UC Berkeley, UC San Diego, UC Irvine, and University of Southern California (USC). And honestly, everything appeared to be a safety school besides Stanford. A "safety school," as described by my college counselor, is a school that you can easily get into based on your numbers. Because my parents had put a lot of pressure on me to get into a good college from an early age and taught me to aim high, I was never concerned about not getting into college. The question was, which one?

Out of the six I had applied to, I *expected* to be accepted by most of them. But my parents would not be happy with that. It wasn't about getting into any college. They told me time and time again; they did not send me to receive a private education to end up at a safety school. They wanted Stanford, and Stanford only.

As I mentioned previously, perhaps too many times, Stanford rejected me. My parents are probably stabbing themselves inside for admitting to the world, that I (once again) did **not** get into Stanford. I merely collected a consolation prize in the Tiger parent world, but would I prove to be an actual failure? I'm going to go with, **no.** The privileges of being a Tiger Cub include being constantly pushed to be the best, and learning to only *want* the best. So I shot for the best, and landed among second best options.

My first acceptance letter was UC Irvine. I'm not hating on any of these colleges or people who attend them, but UC Irvine was not a shocker for me. When I received the acceptance, I tossed it aside and my parents laughed. They had placed me in their honors program, but I was completely uninterested. It was a backup. And when UC San Diego and USC acceptances rolled in, I had the same response. Despite all of the schools offering me money, my parents didn't care. Frankly, it would not be good enough for them. We all know the stereotypes tied to USC, so I'll leave it at that.

The game changer was my acceptance to UC Berkeley. My mom forced me to visit, assuring me that I would love it, but mostly kept repeating that it is the second highest ranked school on my list. Too bad, I hated it. I could not see myself fitting in, and my dad got a $75 parking ticket. Pass.

Through process of elimination, you can probably figure out where I ended up. Yes, I chose to be a UCLA Bruin, and I was a Bruin for free. Free? Yes, all of those years of extra tutoring, private schooling, extra curricular activities, finally paid off. Literally. Giving my parents a big financial break, by attending a fairly top university for free, is something I will forever be proud of.

The biggest privilege of being raised as a Tiger Cub is the luxury of not having to ever worry about your future. All these years, your parents have done the worrying for you, pushed you to your limits, and it was all worth it. While others were waiting on acceptances from these schools, **I had choices**. Though it was no Stanford, it was a hell of a lot cheaper, and we Asians love a good bargain.

Although your parents may show you off like some sort of trophy, ultimately you're the winner of a great education.

9 PICKING A MAJOR

Choosing a Major & Career

What happens after a college accepts you? Are you finally free from your parents' pressure and wishes? You're funny. Of course not. You have four main choices.

Let's start with the most obvious, *pre-med*:

I'm going to lump pre-dent, pre-pharm, pre-optometry all in the same category, as they have similar major requirements. However, be aware that pre-med students are elitist. You may call yourself a doctor in the future, but they sure won't, unless you have the letters M and D after your name.

First of all, can I just clarify that "pre-med" **is not** a major. Pre-med is short for pre-medical, as in you're a pre-medical student. You can't major in being a student. So stop telling people you're majoring in "pre-med." By doing so, you're placing a giant sign on your face that says, "I'm stupid but I want to be your doctor." For the record, you are "pre-med." You don't major in it.

As a pre-medical student, typically you'll major in the following subjects: Anything that starts or ends with "Biology," or "Sciences." They don't call it a B.S. for nothing. Choosing a major is one thing, succeeding in it is another. Here's the problem you'll encounter as a science major, almost every one is a science major. Plus, people think they're hot shit the minute they decide they're going to save lives for their career. Reality check, 80% of people who enter as a "pre-med" student, will not apply to medical school. So put that syringe down and step away from your lab partner, you thirsty pre-med. Pretty much everyone that is pre-med is looking to kill you. Irony at its finest.

Pros: You get to tell people to call you doctor, and you get to save lives. Hell yeah.

Cons: You thought your whole life was one big competition? Being a pre-med student at a top tier college is like playing in the big leagues. If you are planning to attend, or have gone to a big university like I did, that first day of your first chemistry class will scar you for life. My best friend and I found ourselves sitting on the fucking floor. Why? Because everyone showed up 30 minutes early to class to get a seat. However, by the second week, you'll find the lecture halls empty because all the pre-meds have returned to their den to podcast and study. The next time you'll see them? At your midterm & final when they're setting the curves.

The pros here are really smothered by cons, and that is not a coincidence. To be pre-med is to understand the concept of sacrificing your happiness and health to help others.

Engineering

For the Tiger Cubs that were born with a calculator in their brain. For those who are able to do mathematics with a bunch of letters and symbols. For the person who understands how forces work. You are one lucky Tiger Cub. While others have struggled, you've always been good at physics and math. Fortunately, the minute you graduate you'll be making more than the general population. Unfortunately, most engineers also graduate with a shit G.P.A because it's *that* difficult. You're welcome for prepping your self-esteem. I know you're used to getting A's, but it's time to get used to getting B's and C's.

Your parents will love that you're an engineer. You have fulfilled one of the promised Asian destinies. You're braggable, and that's what matters. They can tell their friends over mahjong that you can build rockets and computers out of soda can parts. 90% of what they say will most likely not be true, but it doesn't matter because you're an engineer and they'll believe anything. To Tiger parents, apparently being an engineer is the equivalent of being a smart magician.

Pros: As an engineering major, you were probably bullied as a child for being the nerd. But honestly, those bullies are probably working for you now. Don't worry. Another pro, if you're not the most attractive person, your salary will sure make up for it. You're going to land a job at an amazing company such as Facebook or Google, and suddenly your popularity and desirability levels will rise. You'll be the cool guy riding the colorful bike at Google, while people like me get kicked off their campus.

Bonus points: If you're a girl, you've landed yourself in the world's smartest sausage fest.

Cons: Unless you bleed physics, you're screwed. Also, you're still a nerd. Your family will also probably ask you to fix their computers, even though you've told them plenty of times you don't work for IT.

Pre-law

You spent your whole life fighting with your parents, so why not make it a career? You've always been good at history, you enjoy reading things like the Constitution, and you're pretty damn logical. Here's a quick test to see if this is for you: Jack, Jane, and Joe are sitting in a row. Where is Debby?

If your first response was "Who's Debby?" law is not for you. On the other hand, if your first response starts with, "The question before us is whether or not Debby was present at the scene..." Law is for you. Disclaimer: Don't get fooled by *Legally Blonde* or *Suits*. If you just want to look professional and carry around a brief case, you are definitely in the wrong field. However, if you enjoy things like jury duty, welcome to law.

Similar to the whole "pre-med" thing, you **cannot** major in "pre-law." The funny thing is, you'll never hear a pre-law student mutter the words, "I'm a pre-law major." Why? Because they can speak English properly. Their future career relies on understanding the English language to properly manipulate the fuck out of you. With that being said, here are the subjects you major in: Political Science, History, and English.

Your parents will either have mixed feelings about you being a lawyer. On the one hand, it's a professional career and again, it's humble braggable. "Oh, my daughter's *just* a lawyer at (insert top law firm here)." On the other hand, they will probably hate that you'll throw around legal jargon whenever you want to confuse them. But hey, you gotta have some perks for reviewing all those case studies. Also, occasionally you'll have that one aunt that thinks you're defending criminals, even though you're in patent law. It just happens.

Pros: You can literally spend your career arguing with people, and you'll get paid for it. Furthermore, if you like smashing on people with memorized facts, this is a dream come true. You'll look super impressive because you can recall cases out of thin air. Lawyers appear to be the most confident, aggressive, and intelligent group of people. Even if you're not super intelligent, you sure as hell can convince a jury you know what you're talking about.

Cons: There's a reason Harvey Spector drinks at least once an episode. This job is so stressful; a stress ball would want to burst at the sight of you. First of all, it involves a dead language aka Latin. If you've ever taken Latin, you'll know how confusing this can get. Secondly, imagine getting yelled at all the time as an associate and being someone's bitch for a good amount of your 20's. Third, regardless of what field of law you go into, your friends will constantly come to you for legal advice.

P.S. Anyone want to be my malpractice lawyer?

Business/Accounting

You like money. When people were playing with Pokémon cards, you were trying to sell them. You're the type that would go to Costco, convince your parents to buy the giant tub of candy, and sell it at school. You're sneaky. You're greedy. Cash rules everything around you. Your level of happiness is based on the numbers in your bank account. You keep a close eye on the stock market. If you're looking to be an investment banker, you're more arrogant than Kobe Bryant.

To be more specific, business is only acceptable for Tiger parents if:

1) Your parents run a business and you've always planned to take over.

2) You want to be an accountant, so you can do their taxes.

3) Your goals are to make tons of money by being the CEO of a company.

4) Investment banking, because your monthly paycheck can buy your parents a house.

What does not count as Tiger parent approved business then?

1) Start-up companies = you're currently broke. That's not okay.

2) PR/Marketing= low pay. As important as marketing is for a company, your parents probably think you float around telling people to buy things.

3) Sales in your parents eyes = You might as well work at Macy's.

4) Pyramid scheme = Your grandma will be broke because she bought 30 bottles of whatever you're selling. Seriously stop prostituting your products to your poor old grandma, you money hungry bitch.

Pros if you fall under the "good" category of business: Money. Money. Oh, did I mention money? This is a major pro for those of you who decided to major in Business, Economics, or accounting.

After all, why else would you major in these fields? If you say some bullshit like "because business interests me," stop kidding yourself. You didn't play Monopoly just because it was "fun," you played to win. Deep down you know you've won the jackpot of high paying jobs and you know you'll be able to afford that Birkin without twerkin. #BallSoHard

Cons: Eventually all that money is going to get boring. What kind of life are you living if you're constantly striving for more money? People are probably going to think you're greedy. If you're an investment banker or involved with the stock market, your life and your happiness literally depends on numbers going up or down. If NASDAQ decided to take a plunge, you bet your client is going to be pissed you just recently bought 10,000 shares. You'll probably take that anger out on your family and kids.

But no worries, you'll wipe away those tears with your hundreds.

Let's Talk Alternatives:

Oh wait, there are none. You want to major in Asian American studies? Geology? Art? Sociology? Unless you're planning on double majoring with one of the possible majors listed above, or you want to get a Ph.D. in your field, think again. In order for your parents to successfully humble brag about you, you have to give them something to brag about. This requires an extra couple letters after your name, i.e. M.D, M.B.A, Ph.D., D.D.S, PharmD, J.D…etc. An additional degree means additional money. Additional money equals additional pride. So, unless you want to get disowned, get your shit together.

Am I An Imposter?

The question now is, where do I fit in? I'm sitting here, claiming to be raised by strict parents, claiming that to be an experienced Tiger Cub, so I should be excelling in one of the four areas of expertise, yet I'm writing a book. So instead of supporting our parents, writers are thought to live at home and eat their food. We're leeches. Did I just completely waste your time? Am I about to just ruin my credibility? Are you pissed that you just read a whole book with a bunch of advice from someone that might be holding a "Spare some change" sign by the freeway?

Here's the thing. I categorized the majors for convenience and for logical purposes. Yes, those who major in something starting or ending with "biology" or "science," will most likely end up being a doctor, dentist, optometrist, researcher, in debt for a good 15-20 years. Yes, those who major in engineering will end up being a rich nerd. Yes, Tiger Cubs who choose to major in Political Science, History or English, will most likely end up being a lawyer. And yes, those who major in business, will be more than happy to have money rule their lives. I'm not denying any of my previous stereotypes.

However, I have never been satisfied falling into a stereotype. I majored in English and I do **not** want to be a lawyer. Nothing about logic games excite me. If you hand me a Sudoku, I'll use it as a coaster. I also mentioned my little anecdote about my best friend and me, sitting on the floor of a chemistry classroom. Was I just keeping her company? No, I took a shit ton of science classes in college. In fact, I was raised as such an overachieving bitch that I majored in English *and* completed my pre-medical requirements. While writing this book, I'm awaiting medical school interviews. While other people were reading scientific journals, I was reading American fiction.

The lesson here is: there's no escaping your Tiger Cub roots. No matter what you pursue, eventually it'll all end up being a professional career. Your parents won't let you starve on the streets; instead they'll make you go to more school. I went into college knowing I wanted to be pre-med, but there was a period of time where I went haywire and switched to business. Even in those moments, I switched between one of the four choices. Then, when I told my parents I wanted to major in English, their faces turned white as a ghost geisha. They were *that* pale. Frankly, they were probably confused as fuck. Doctors major in science. Lawyers major in English.

So, for those of you who want some advice in changing your major, make sure to always please your Tiger parents. What did I go with? "I'm majoring with English because I'll stand out in my medical school application." Do I know that for sure? Hell no. In fact, English taught me to B.S. so much, sometimes I convince myself I'm telling the truth. The key is to always turn it back to what your parents would want. It's called a compromise.

Let me help you out:

You want to major in art? "I really enjoy art, and it'll be especially useful to familiarize myself with colors...colors of pills, when I become a pharmacist."

You want to major in geology? "Don't worry, I'll get my Ph.D. and you can tell your friends I have a doctorate."

You want to major in sociology? Chances are your parents have no idea what sociology is, so spin it however you want to.

Tiger parents will hear what they want to hear, so slip in "doctor," "lawyer," or any other respectable professional job and I'm sure you'll be fine. Before you decide to bend the rules, just remember they feed and house you. Plus, here's a perk of choosing a professional career: you'll have more time in grad school to lollygag.

10 CONCLUSION: THE PRIVILEGES

"Haters going to hate, hate, hate," says Taytay Swift. And yes, you'll have your haters. People who will call you an overachiever, people who will say you're doing too much, people who question your parents' "techniques." Plus, even though I'm sure there are people who have a shit ton to say about this book, I don't care. You read it. You know my point of view, feel free to share or disagree with it. At the end of the day while you were sitting around eating chips, I was sitting around eating chips and writing a book. And don't even start with the exceptions to the stereotypes, because everything in life has its exceptions. I'm not about to write you a 500-page novel covering all the bases. This is a briefing on the Tiger Cub life, a fun read, a relatable story for those who have been or are currently being raised like I was as a child. Of course I can go on and on about the potential careers or other potential majors that are acceptable for Asians, but ain't nobody got time for that.

I'm not stupid. I know this might have offended people who attended shit colleges like UC Merced, but I warned you from the beginning; this isn't for the light hearted. This book was written for those who were raised as strong individuals. To you sensies (sensitive people), I told you to peace out. Originally, the book was written with zero disclaimers. Why should I have to explain myself or justify why I'm writing in a certain way? But for you pansies, overcritical, jealous beezies, I compromised, kind of.

CONFESSIONS OF A TIGER CUB

A lot of my stories are anecdotes. For those who haven't studied their SAT vocabulary yet, anecdotes are *personal* stories; they're meant to be short and amusing. If I wanted to write a memoir, I would. But frankly, I'm not a big enough narcissist or else I would've chosen to be a fashion blogger. I hope you've been able to relate to these anecdotes or maybe even thought of your own warm, fuzzy memories of getting buried under sheet music.

Despite all the punishments, the disciplining, and the extra homework while other children were playing outside, 22 years later, I appreciate it all. My parents and my grandparents gave me everything and still give me everything to help me succeed. Yes, they gave me the material goods, or whatever you would call SAT prep books, but I have been raised with certain personality quirks only Tiger Cubs seem to possess.

Career Oriented & Goal Perks:

My anaconda don't. My anaconda don't. My anaconda don't want none if you're flippin' burger buns, hun. Unless you got a stable career, an "interesting" relationship with your parents, or you went through the same shit I did, we can't be friends. Why? It's all about compatibility. When have you ever seen someone ambitious, successful, and beautiful...ending up with a minimum wage worker? Please. Tiger Cubs are raised with the following:

Elitist attitude:
So what, you're a little elitist. You believe you can't settle for anything less than the best. You look down on those who haven't worked as hard as you, because you know how much you have put into your own success. Being elitist sometimes has a negative connotation. It is often confused with being condescending, but let me just stop you right there. Your elitist attitude does **not** need to be expressed. No one is telling you to run around shitting on people who are below you. Although that would be a hilarious site, your parents taught you

better than that.

Having an elitist attitude is internal. Unfortunately, because you were never good enough for your parents, other people are never good enough for you either. Someone tells you, "oh my friend is making $60k a year!" You have every right to think, "So what?" Deep down, you know you can do better, you'll be making 3 times that salary, and you'll continue striving for it.

Speaking of salary, being an elitist beezy requires you to marry someone equally elitist. If you're making $250k a year, your parents are expecting your future husband to make equal or more than that. Luckily for you, your elitist husband will probably want someone equally capable, but still making less (to fuel his manhood). With that being said, it isn't purely about gender norms, but more about aiming for someone above you. If you can't make more, then marry the person that can. It's all about survival of the fittest, and you want the fittest and richest mate. My Tiger mom has always said, "Find someone that can give you the option to quit your job." Forget "true love," no one is good enough for you unless they can provide eternal financial support for you and your family.

In case you still haven't gotten the point, there is nothing wrong with being elitist. It's okay to think highly of yourself. If you are confident in your abilities, you'll show it through your success. By comparing yourself to others, you learn to better yourself and continue rising. If we lived in a world with no rank, where would the motivation be? Stay impressive. Stay elitist. Stay above the norm.

Ambition:
From an early age, we were taught to be the best. Often times, other people may call you an overachiever. People may question how you had time to play all those instruments, sports, build a shelter, and still manage to earn straight A's. The answer, you and your parents made time. I don't know about you, but laziness is my #1 pet peeve. Seeing smart people waste away their day by sleeping or not trying in

school, is insulting when you have busted your ass your whole life. But really, that's none of my business.

Being ambitious is an amazing feeling. It keeps you from working those fast food, minimum wage jobs. It sets higher standards for you. It lets you believe you can accomplish anything you put your mind to. I have always looked for my next goal, my next accomplishment, and it has kept me from plateauing. Although you may often fail in your endeavors, staying ambitious will prevent the downward spiral.

A huge part of why I decided to write a book was because waiting for medical school interviews had literally started to drive me crazy. There were nights when I was self-diagnosed with insomnia. Thoughts about failing, not getting into medical school, started to plague my everyday life. I found myself unable to focus on work, unable to ever have a clear mind, and I knew I needed to find a solution. I couldn't be sleepless forever.

The easy way out would have been to continue staying in my own head, continue having this eternal medical school process eat away at me for the next year. If I were lazy, I would probably buy Dramamine and just knock myself out every night. But, ambitious people find real solutions. My self-esteem started to be dictated by my progress with my applications and I was done feeling sorry for myself. I was tired of feeling useless, as though my years of research, my publications, and my torturous school nights, were getting me nowhere in life. I knew I had to find a long-term solution, a new source of motivation.

I asked myself, "What could I do to be useful?" I knew I had to find another outlet of inspiration and incentive to succeed in any field. So, I decided to put my original major, English, to use. After tutoring the kids, I realized how lucky they were to also have such caring parents. Of course their parents were the dictionary definition of "Tiger parents," but these kids were conditioned to compete and care from an early age, whether they knew it or not. There is a reason I dedicated a full chapter to my tutoring experience. It definitely isn't because I love kids (let's go back and count how many times I said I wanted to adopt an adult). However, these kids reflected the importance of my own parents' teachings.

My parents raised me to believe I could do anything I put my mind to. In my dad's eyes, "anything" slowly started to turn into "medicine." Why? Pursuing medicine is a sign of ambition, intelligence and self-sacrifice. Even though I found my own motivations throughout various experiences in college and with my family, I kept those characteristics in mind to pursue any of my goals. The ambition I had to write this book, the intelligence I trick people into believing I have, and the self-sacrifice of deciding to publish this book on top of my two jobs I currently work.

Also, not to mention the self-sacrificial ceremony that will take place when I tell my parents I wrote this or actually used my English degree. The horror, the horror.

Bonus points: if you can name the reference listed above.

Non-Academic Perks

Discipline/Good Manners:
First of all, not all Asian kids are raised equally. There is a huge difference between Asian kids who were raised the Tiger parent way, and other kids. My mom recently told me a middle school child at her church was blowing his nose and throwing tissues on the ground. Animal. If I had done that as a child, I would be slapped so hard, I'd be on my pile of dirty tissues. Being a loud crier at a restaurant, would only buy me time in house-jail. Tiger parents condition their children to behave; and after seeing how other kids behave, holy shit, thank you, mom & dad.

Children strongly reflect their parents when it comes to discipline and good manners. The "they're just kids" excuse is far from excusable. Tiger Cubs, or those who were trained, are extremely well behaved. When you see an elder, you greet them. Not only do you greet them by saying a simple, "hello," you greet them with their full title and relationship to you, and you follow it with "I hope you are well." You say everything you can to make sure the level of respect is there, or else you know what'll happen next. Your funeral.

I will never forget the days (yes, multiple) I was verbally assaulted by my mom for the following: Not greeting people loudly enough for them to hear, not knowing the relationship I had to refer to someone to as, not saying "thank you and I hope you are healthy and prosperous" when receiving a red envelope, when I signed an e-mail without addressing her properly, asking if my mom was coming to my piano exam, or telling her I was not hungry. At the time, none of these seemed like a big deal. I thought I spoke loudly enough, I didn't know I had to shout at my elders. I thought she was my aunt, I didn't know her name changes when she marries into the family. I thought "thank you" was enough. I didn't know my mom would flip a bitch when I casually signed my e-mails. I definitely should not have rushed her to enter the piano exam building, even though we were already 5 minutes late. I didn't know telling her I wasn't hungry right now, would lead to no dinner at all. **My bad.**

Sass does not cut it for Tiger parents. Depending on your parents' moods, everything that comes out of your mouth could be filled with "attitude" you did not know you had. Suddenly, talking to them becomes "talking back." And don't even try the "I didn't know," card. It will feed into the angry downward spiral you have already started. Soon every defense you can think of will be answered with "it's common sense." You'll be at a loss of words because clearly it was not common sense to you, but you'll learn to let it go. Although each of my examples was given for different mistakes, they all started with my ignorance, and ended with lots of tears.

The minute you start apologizing for things you did not even know you could apologize for, is the minute you have given up. Seriously, stop fighting with your parents. About 5 years post-puberty, you'll realize all the verbal lashing will turn you into the most well-mannered adult while meeting your Tiger mom's friends. They'll comment about how polite you are, knowing that it was probably beaten into you. That is your shining moment. In your professional life, you'll be more than comfortable meeting strangers, because you've been addressing a ton of strangers as your "aunts" and "uncles" your whole life. During an interview, you will be more than aware of social cues and etiquette. You might have to find another outlet for your sass, but that's what your friends are for.

Sheltered: Literally and metaphorically.

Literally, right out of college, you have nowhere to go. Fuck. You just spent 4 years of your life, trying to figure out what to do, and now you have to go home and tell your parents that you need a year off to apply to your next step. Or the alternative, you have a job and it happens to be close to home, but you don't make enough to leave your nest. Your parents will house you. No problem, no questions asked. Well, maybe some questions, everyday, about your life progress.

Unlike college, where it might have been ridiculously annoying to cook for yourself or beg people for "swipes" to the dining halls, coming home is a blessing in disguise. Yes, if you are a girl, you'll revert back to a 16 year old in high school with a curfew. But, let's not forget the other perks of being 16 aka laundry and free food. There is nothing you'll appreciate more than a home cooked meal and a roof over your head. The money you make from your job will go toward your gas money and whatever fun necessities you want, because your parents are still paying your bills and health insurance. Hell yeah. Be appreciative.

Metaphorically, your parents will always shelter you from the "bad" in the world. How many times has your mom still told you to put on a jacket, when it's about 70 degrees out? How many times has your dad asked you if you've eaten yet? No matter how old you are, your parents will always be the over-protective, worriers. Although sometimes you may feel like you're drowning in their love, your parents are constantly going to support you with the contingency that you are going to show them you're about to achieve greatness. After all, no one is going to sponsor a loser.

Your parents continue to be protective because they have pretty much raised you to be the perfect version of what they want. You have become a prized gem. Imagine spending 18 years developing, crafting, molding, investing in a small business, and finally being able to see the benefits slowly come in aka when you get accepted to a top 20 college. There is no way your parents are going to let their personal money ball run loose. They'll keep a careful eye on your success, because in another 20 years, you'll be more than happy and able to pay them back via new Mercedes.

Win-win.

Life Lessons Learned

All right, it's time to get sentimental. Honestly, there are no hard feelings if you close this book and never look at it again. You don't have to read the last few pages if you feel at peace with yourself. But if you want to hear some of my mushier nonsense, here we go. Now that everything is said and done with, what should you take out of this? First and foremost, be thankful. Be thankful your parents didn't spoil you with materialistic goods, but with their undying care and attention. Be thankful you were never that annoying screaming baby on an airplane. Be thankful your parents raised you to be ambitious. Be thankful you'll never be the one to settle for less. Be thankful you will always be housed, fed, and loved.

I've admitted many times that our upbringing may be out of the "norm." I'm pretty sure people didn't get smacked for silly things like not completing sentences when greeting someone. However, I'm positive we're all going to be the same with our future kids because all of the discipline seemed to have worked on us. Although many of us joke about going through "child abuse," there is nothing *actually* abusive about how we were raised. We learn quickly, we behave better, and we are pushed to be our best.

Writing this book/novella/whatever you want to call it, has been a journey of self-reflection and more importantly a comedic approach to our upbringing. If you are a Tiger Cub yourself, you were most likely able to laugh at relatable stories, or recall some of your own. If you were not a Tiger Cub, you now know that Asian parenting techniques aren't as bad as people make them out to be. They're harsh, but they work. Everything we go through is a privilege. Having parents that love and care for you is something people constantly take for granted.

No matter how much they yell at you, or take away your toys, or make you question why you're still living, they will constantly support you. After seeing countless misbehaved animal children roaming restaurants and low life teenagers wasting away their education, I started to realize that the real privileges include the values our parents instill in us and our drive to succeed. This book is proof that you can do anything you set your mind to. It is also proof that being an English major doesn't equal being homeless. Whatever your actual major is, I'm positive you can spin it in a way to be successful. If not, proceed to pick one of the four Tiger parent approved careers.

All of our experiences make up who we are today, and that sure isn't a bad thing. Continue to be thankful. Continue to cherish the benefits. And lastly, continue to carry those Tiger Cub personality traits wherever you go.

ABOUT THE AUTHOR

Jenny Lin is an alumna of the University of California, Los Angeles with her Bachelors of Arts degree in English. Raised in a Taiwanese household, she comically portrays her experience as an Asian American going through early childhood until present day. Sarcastic and witty, she communicates the struggles, but more importantly, the appreciation she has for her parents. With the recent term *Tiger Mom* becoming popularized, she recognized a need to illustrate the child's perspective in a positive light. Not only is she an author of her first novella, *Confessions of a Tiger Cub*, she has also authored multiple publications in various acclaimed scientific journals. Her versatility allows for a broad scope of different experiences Asian American teens may face, before and after college. Brutally honest, sassy and occasionally sweet, she writes with an open heart for her readers.

Made in the USA
Columbia, SC
01 May 2023